Outdoor Rooms
Fresh Air Kitchens and Living Areas

Tina Skinner &
Melissa Cardona

Schiffer Publishing Ltd

4880 Lower Valley Road, Atglen, PA 19310

Other Schiffer Books by Tina Skinner & Melissa Cardona

Fire Outdoors: Fireplaces, Fire Pits & Cook Centers

Creative Patios

Pools, Patios, and Fabulous Outdoor Living Spaces: Luxury by Master Pool Builders

Master Built Pools & Patios: An Inspiring Portfolio of Design Ideas

Hot Tubs & Spas: An Inspirational Design Guide

Pure Deck-adence

All Decked Out...Redwood Decks: Ideas and Plans for Contemporary Outdoor Living

The Deck Book

Paver Projects: Designs For Amazine Outdoor Environments

Retaining Walls

Other Schiffer Books on Related Subjects

Petite Patios & Intimate Garden Spaces

The Patio Portfolio: An Inspirational Design Guide

Patios, Driveways, and Plazas: The Pattern Language of Concrete Pavers

Backyards & Boulevards: A Portfolio of Concrete Paver Projects

Acknowledgements

Thanks to Nathaniel Wolfgang-Price, who contributed significantly to the production of this book.

Special thanks to Worldwise of Marin County, California, for allowing us to reprint their essay on choosing Environmentally friendly materials for outdoor furnishings.

Designed by "Sue"
Type set in Novarese Bk BT/Souvenir Lt BT

ISBN: 978-0-7643-2459-8
Printed in China

Schiffer Books are available at special discounts for bulk purchases for sales promotions or premiums. Special editions, including personalized covers, corporate imprints, and excerpts can be created in large quantities for special needs. For more information contact the publisher:

Published by Schiffer Publishing Ltd.
4880 Lower Valley Road
Atglen, PA 19310
Phone: (610) 593-1777; Fax: (610) 593-2002
E-mail: Info@schifferbooks.com

For the largest selection of fine reference books on this and related subjects, please visit our website at:
www.schifferbooks.com
We are always looking for people to write books on new and related subjects. If you have an idea for a book please contact us at the above address.

This book may be purchased from the publisher.
Include $5.00 for shipping.
Please try your bookstore first.
You may write for a free catalog.

In Europe, Schiffer books are distributed by
Bushwood Books
6 Marksbury Ave.
Kew Gardens
Surrey TW9 4JF England
Phone: 44 (0) 20 8392 8585; Fax: 44 (0) 20 8392 9876
E-mail: info@bushwoodbooks.co.uk
Website: www.bushwoodbooks.co.uk

Contents

Extending the Home Outward

The Porch

In western minds, the porch is a place of arrival on the front of the home, the place of retreat on the back. A porch is an extension of the home, sometimes with a separate roof, often sheltered on the overhang of the main structure's eaves. Town folk greet their neighbors from the front porch, and invite them aboard for a glass of iced tea. We entice our visitors inside to move outside with us, stepping out to the back porch where we take our meals whenever the weather permits.

A porch is generally open to the elements, though it may have half walls, or screened panels to shelter it from insects. In our fantasies, it is furnished with a swing, or studded with rocking chairs where we gently soothe ourselves to the sounds of nature.

Generally, a porch is raised above ground level, and covered with a ceiling, but is open on one or more sides. It may be screened in for protection from insects, and porches are often "enclosed" as a new addition to the home itself. A small porch may be referred to as a "stoop" or sheltered "portico" referring to its

On a lazy summer's day, when the afternoon winds down, the front porch becomes the perfect place to go where a person can have a cup of tea and a biscuit, flip through a magazine, or just sit back in a rocking chair and relax. *Courtesy of Laneventure*

role as an entryway to the home. An extensive stretch of porch is sometimes referred to as a "veranda," though this term can also apply to raised balconies.

Left: A warm, golden ceiling and cool stone floors set the stage for outdoor dining in this open-air space. *Courtesy of Gloster Furniture, Inc.*

An assortment of lounge chairs and upright slings make lingering on the front porch more attractive. *Courtesy of Winston Furniture*

Pillow Talk

Bring upholstered pieces outdoors on the weekends, or let them live on your porch all summer. Textiles not only add color, they add layers of comfort. The softer the seat, the more apt you are to linger and feel at home sitting outside.

Festive candy striped cushions give this back porch a slight holiday air, with the added fun element of glider mechanisms under much of the seating. *Courtesy of Winston Furniture*

Warm shades of brown accented with soft cream create a cozy atmosphere enhanced by warm sunshine and fresh air. *Courtesy of Yvonne Gregory Interiors, LLC*

Green furnishings accented with crisp white give this spacious back porch a feeling of "natural" energy. *Courtesy of Yvonne Gregory Interiors, LLC*

An octagonal porch extension provides arched views from comfortably sheltered seating. *Courtesy of Carter Grandle*

Fluffy cushions and bright white wicker await beachgoers retreating from the sun to this cool, ocean-front verandah. *Courtesy of Laneventure*

Made for lovers, or best friends, a porch joins two in a repetitive sweep. *Courtesy of Telescope Casual Furniture, Inc.*

Spacious enough for twenty, an outdoor porch is all the more luxurious when enjoyed by one. *Courtesy of Telescope Casual Furniture, Inc.*

Above and left: In this porch extension, arches are the primary architectural feature. *Courtesy of Harrison Design Associates*

Loggia

An Italian word and sensibility, loggia are galleries that hug the ground-level of a home, their roofs supported by columns, and their views to the exterior generally framed by arches. Part and parcel of any Mediterranean-style home, these arcades create a transition between indoors and out, and are often furnished for daily living. They are the colonnaded passageways between home and courtyard, providing shade, shelter, and usually elegant structure to the outdoor environment.

Top: Loggia stretch the length of two wings of this house, sheltering a water-filled courtyard. Wood columns give this Spanish Revival home structure its Southwestern flair, perfect for an Arizona abode. *Courtesy of Patio Pools of Tucson, Inc.*

Bottom: Glazed bricks make up the floor in this Mediterranean-style loggia, where the warm climate makes outdoor activities possible year-round. Grecian columns topped with composite capitals give the space a classic touch. *Courtesy of Brown Jordan*

The arch was frequently found in the architecture of the Ancient Romans who were the first people to use an arch above ground. Here, a series of arches not only supports the weight of two porches, they also open up into two outdoor rooms. *Courtesy of Harrison Design Associates*

Weathered bricks give this space a sense of antiquity and dignity, while the furnishings promise contemporary comfort. *Courtesy of Telescope Casual Furniture, Inc.*

An outdoor room gets warmth from copper- and brick-colored furnishings. *Courtesy of O.W. Lee, Inc.*

Loggia

Right: Two tones in the stucco finish accent the architecture in this expansive loggia. Comfortable furnishings emphasize the everyday use of the space. *Courtesy of Winston Furniture*

Below: Spaciousness allows room for cooking, dining, and lounging fireside afterward. *Courtesy of McGarvey Custom Homes*

A ground floor loggia framed in stone arches provides an Old World atmosphere for family gatherings. A kitchen area and bar, complete with a television, are among the amenities of the space. *Courtesy of Harrison Design Associates*

A brick-faced loggia functions as an outdoor living room. A dedicated alcove emphasizes the importance of the barbecue in this family's summer menu plan. *Courtesy of Harrison Design Associates*

Totem-like wooden sculptures stand sentinel in arched entrances to a loggia. Within, curtains draw back to reveal kitchen and dining areas opulent in their décor. *Courtesy of Harrison Design Associates*

Lanai

What better place for an outdoor living room than Hawaii? So it comes as no surprise that there is a Hawaiian word for just such a space. A lanai is not restricted to any architectural style, but simply implies that the room is open in part or in whole to the outdoors. In many cases, and in places where the outdoors is not always so clement, pocket doors can be opened to create a lanai.

A decorative valance adorns the entrance to an indoor/outdoor salon. Orchids and a tropical print emphasize the ideal climate for this California lanai. *Courtesy of Susan Cohen Associates, Inc.*

Double sets of French doors can be flung wide open to admit the cool sea breezes to this indoor/outdoor room. *Courtesy of Brown Jordan*

Photos by Carol Newman

Pocket doors allow a glass wall to be drawn to the corners of this open lanai, to block wind or add privacy. The owners enjoy open views to the sea, mountains, and their exquisite garden. A wooden bridge links the house to a rock garden, where a bamboo fence adds Asian sensibility to a space imbued with comfort and tranquility. *Courtesy of Brian Higley, Landscape Architect*

Glass pocket doors slide away, eliminating the barrier between this living room and a loggia. *Courtesy of KAA Design Group*

Curtains part on a stage-like entrance to reveal an outdoor kitchen and living area, furnished with tables, chairs, a pull-out television, and a bar. The curtains can be drawn to darken the room for film screenings or when not in use. *Courtesy of Susan Cohen Associates, Inc.*

Whether it's formal dining with guests or a casual bite to eat, this large lanai is the place to do it. *Courtesy of McGarvey Custom Homes*

Above: A back-porch hideaway, cleanly furnished, is the perfect spot to catch up on reading while enjoying the fresh air. *Courtesy of Gloster Furniture, Inc.*

Right: Circular bench seating is easily tucked away, or pulled further out to accommodate one more diner. *Courtesy of Telescope Casual Furniture, Inc.*

Balconies and Rooftops

Depending on how your home is designed, walking out a door at ground level isn't always convenient. Balconies have been around for centuries to offer those dwelling above the frost line an easy out to the fresh air. Today's homes are often equipped with raised decks and verandas that serve the same purpose – making it easy to transport a piping hot meal to a table situated *al fresco*, or for someone just arising from slumber to slip outside and test the air.

For city dwellers, an above ground surface may offer their only opportunity to create a living space outdoors. Rooftops and balconies double as nature retreats for the concrete clad urbanite, a chance to grow container gardens and strain for a note of distant birdsong.

Practicality aside, what could be better than a bird's-eye perch among the tree-tops? It's the outdoors with a much loftier perspective.

Gauzy curtains and French doors open to reveal a spacious balcony, formally furnished in cappuccino colored wicker and upholstery designed to withstand the elements. The ideal perch with a commanding view has universal appeal, whether one is surveying rooftops, a seashore, or mountain scenery. *Courtesy of Gloster Furniture, Inc.*

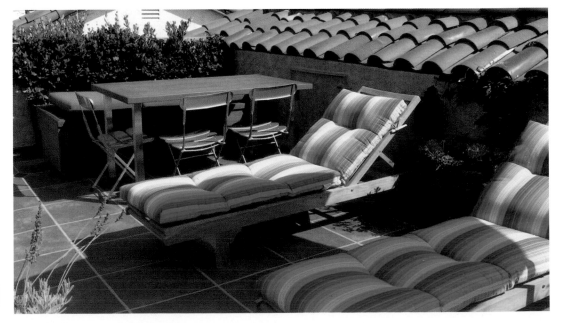

On a rooftop escape, bright blues and greens add cool to the Southwestern tile roof and patio. A bench serves as convenient storage for cushions when not in use. *Courtesy of Park Slope Design*

Two angular seating areas jut out from this balcony, adding visual interest and additional space. Two framed trellises have been wired for climbing plants, which will soon help bring the garden atmosphere up to the second floor. *Courtesy of the California Redwood Association*

Cast aluminum patio furniture creates an intimate dining space on a second floor balcony. *Courtesy of Tropitone*

Above left: A tropical floral pattern on the footstool and accent pillows adds a playful note to this lush balcony retreat. *Courtesy of Laneventure*

Above right: Jutting out from the second floor, a balcony offers solitude, an opportunity to sit and relax, and a wonderful view of the surrounding property. *Courtesy of Harrison Design Associates*

Left: Blue, green, and white stripes add nautical notes to a second-floor balcony. *Courtesy of Carter Grandle*

A rooftop spa and deck were created for homeowners, and frosted glass was put in place to provide privacy. *Courtesy of David Gast & Associates*

Moving Away from the House

Above: An arched wooden gate is a focal point for this pretty patio, where casual furniture awaits the command of occupants with regard to arrangement. *Courtesy of Tropitone*

Below: Of necessity, a courtyard often offered the home's inhabitants a watering hole – generally a place where drinking and cooking water was stored. The Romans perfected this aspect into an aesthetic, with a long trough that served as a reflecting pool, as well as providing sustenance. Here the element is expanded for bathing, surrounded by sheltered areas where the family members can lounge, cook, and dine outdoors. *Courtesy of Toll Brothers*

The Courtyard

The courtyard is an integral part of architectural history, from castle keeps to the genteel family areas of Mediterranean homes, to the central living areas among the masses of Asian homes. Carefully shielded by walls and buildings, courtyards create a sense of privacy and safety where a family can conduct their affairs.

In the West, the courtyards came to the country with a strong Spanish heritage. Walled courtyard enclosures are part and parcel of the Spanish Revival homes that dot North America and dominate the Southern and Westernmost states. Architects have adapted the courtyard to other schools of design, using walls, el building formations, and other creative devices to provide the same enclosed sense for outdoor spaces.

Stucco walls cozied next to the home with a shade-giving arbor recreates the classic Mediterranean courtyard ambiance. *Courtesy of Tropitone*

A heating unit makes the Mediterranean ideal of courtyard living more accessible to those in Northern climates. This propane lamp provides both light and heat to an outdoor space. Around the base, small vents release heat and on the top a gas-powered lamp sheds light around the space. *Courtesy of Empire Comfort Systems, Inc.*

Surrounded by lush foliage, a courtyard lounge is a small oasis of calm in the middle of an active household. A leaf pattern on the seat cushions unites the appearance of the "room." *Courtesy of Winston Furniture*

A courtyard setting serves as a family room when weather allows. Lightweight furnishings allow family members and friends to rearrange the "room" at a whim. *Courtesy of Brown Jordan*

Straight lines and simple colors add a modern twist to the courtyard scene, harmonizing for an air of tranquility and peace found in this contemporary outdoor living space. The furnishings add modern comfort to the setting, with thick cushions upholstered in special textiles designed to withstand weather. *Courtesy of Sutherland and Perennials Outdoor Fabrics*

The home, a shed, and the landscaping work together to enclose a space reminiscent of the classic courtyard. The desired effect being one of cozy privacy in the open air.

A wooden privacy fence and shed enclose a comfortable backyard nook. Rustic elements – bent willow furniture and a rough-cut granite fire bowl – give this outdoor room a homey feeling. *Courtesy of David Bartsch*

Open courtyards like these are frequently found in the Mediterranean, where the weather is warm most of the year and outside activities are frequent. *Courtesy of Scott Zucker*

A small basement walkout is magnified using mirrored panels. Movable containers allow the bamboo to be shifted about, and taunt wires were incorporated to train climbing plants and, in short time, provide privacy from prying eyes above. *Courtesy of Julia Fogg, Landscape Architect*

Glossary of Backyard Structures

Arbor – initially defined as an open structure of trees or shrubs closely planted, either self-supporting or twined together on a latticework frame. The term has evolved to include wooden structures, usually built as an open framework of wood beams, left open or used to train climbing plants. Used interchangeably with the term trellis.

Colonnade – a number of columns arranged at intervals. Though these may be simply capped with an entablature, the colonnade is generally used to support one side of a roof.

Courtyard – an open area partially or fully enclosed by buildings or other walls, adjacent to or within a home or other building.

Folly – an eye-catching structure, often without function, that originated for ornament of English estate gardens. Often they were built to imitate a ruin, or to highlight a view.

Gazebo – a summerhouse where the walls have been left open to afford views in several or all directions.

Lanai – a living room or lounge area left in part or entirely open to the outdoors.

Loggia – an arcaded or colonnaded porch or gallery attached to a larger structure, open on one or more sides.

Pavilion – a structure used for entertainment, usually characterized by a special roof forms, characteristically central projections. May be a temporary structure or tent.

Pergola – a building, even a lean-to, built beyond the main home and used to shade a walk or passageway. In landscape terminology, these are generally decorative garden structures, often latticed and supported by regularly spaced posts or columns.

Porch – a structure added to a building to shelter an entrance or to serve as a semi-enclosed space, usually roofed and generally open-sided.

Portal – an impressive or monumental entryway to a building, doorway, or courtyard.

Portico – A porch or covered walk consisting of a roof supported by columns, or a free-standing, roofed colonnade.

Ramada – A Spanish word for arbor, these open structures may stand alone or be attached to a building, and have solid roofs.

Trellis – a latticework of metal or wood used to support vines. The term has come to be interchangeable with arbors.

Trellis

One of the simplest outdoor structures can be the trellis – either a panel or a structure made of grating or latticework. With its roots firmly entrenched in the garden, trellis structures evolved from designs created to support plants. However, they have come to exist as elements independent of greenery in many backyard settings. Beautiful trellis structures are just that – sculptural things of beauty built primarily as focal points for outdoor settings. Though they may provide some shade to those who gather beneath, trellis principally work to define gathering spaces as they afford little to no shelter from the elements.

Above and left: Warm lights emanate from the dominant view of this classic trelliswork gazebo. *Courtesy of Memphis Pools*

A trellised roofline creates an open-air porch beside a contemporary home. *Courtesy of KAA Design Group*

A trellis over this seating area helps to filter sunlight. A built in barbeque makes meals on the patio easy. *Courtesy of Oldcastle Architectural, Inc.*

In a contemporary take on the trellis, massive concrete beams support the more delicate wood lattice above. Trellis slats filter the light and add dramatic shadows to this contemporary space. Futuristic chairs and table complement their clean-cut stucco surroundings. *Courtesy of Brown Jordan*

A garden room, shaded by a trellis, offers a table and a set of chairs for a quiet getaway. *Courtesy of Gib-San Pools*

Here redwood decking was used to construct an impressive elevated gathering area crowned by a wooden trellis. *Courtesy of the California Redwood Association*

An arbor extends the home across portions of this cascading patio. A waterfall and goldfish pond add tranquility and beauty to the space. Away from the back patio and the goldfish pond, a table and chairs have been placed on this section of the patio to take advantage of the view over the lawn. *Courtesy of Dan Berger, LandPlan Landscaping*

Water cascades over natural rocks into a kidney shaped spa. A gathering area was created amidst a horseshoe-shaped half wall, sheltered by a winged trellis. Close by, a grill, bar, and fireplace await family and guests. *Courtesy of Creative Master Pools*

A carved antique wooden headboard adds an interesting decorative element to an outdoor patio. *Courtesy of Harrison Design Associates*

For a sophisticated, Old World dining experience outdoors, a table has been placed underneath a vine-covered trellis on an old brick patio. The deep green color of the wicker furniture compliments the color of the surrounding foliage. *Courtesy of Laneventure*

Pergola

A deck-top pergola invites the garden aboard. Within a few years, plants and wood will combine to create a lush shaded place where the family can congregate. *Courtesy of Casa Decks*

Surrounded by climbing vines, the pergola provides structure, privacy, and shade for a comfortable dining room. *Courtesy of Park Slope Design*

Besides being decorative, vines like the ones growing up the pergola and on the side of the house serve to add a feeling of age and dignity to a newer patio. *Courtesy of Park Slope Design*

Above: Vines obscure the wood structure of a pergola, enriching the shaded space beneath. *Courtesy of Tropitone*

Right: A trellised extension creates an outdoor space, in this case spacious enough to serve as many rooms for occupants who want a breath of fresh air. *Courtesy of Laneventure*

Above right and right: Wire mesh and steel rods will add structure to vines, making for a shaded approach to this home in the near future. *Courtesy of Dan Berger, LandPlan Landscaping*

A mat of greenery fills in the spaces between this pergola, creating an organic roof for this small pavilion.

A picnic pavilion stands separate from the patio and the house, tempting with shade and refreshment for those who make the journey. *Courtesy of MarcoDesigns and Alfresco Designs*

Pavilion

Defined as a structure used for entertaining, pavilions can be temporary or permanent. Temporary tents, called pavilions, have leant their shape to the standard four-cornered pavilion envisioned today at first mention of the word. However, in today's lexicon, the term pavilion generally implies a large, open structure true to its roots – designed for entertaining. More often than not, pavilions are supported roofs, completely open on the sides. In parks and other public spaces, pavilions shelter picnic areas. Likewise, in a residential setting, they are designed as shade and shelter set amidst the open landscape.

Dried chilies hanging underneath the edge of this pavilion's roof along with various desert plants emphasize this backyard's place in the Southwestern landscape. *Courtesy of Joe Murray Landscapes*

Benches, bridges, and backyard buildings become destinations, motivation to move outdoors and linger beyond. *Courtesy of Harrison Design Associates*

A backyard pavilion was fashioned to function as a dream kitchen for an avid grill chef. Fencing provides privacy walls for the suburban setting, where friends and family frequently gather to enjoy company, fresh air, and the fruits of the owner's culinary labor. *Courtesy of Remodeling Services*

A pavilion built to impress was placed poolside, big enough to play host to ranks of important guests. *Courtesy of Harrison Design Associates*

A pavilion overlooks a meandering pool environment, where spa waters spill through a rock border into the swimming area below. Flagstone is used on the walkways and walls in this luxurious backyard landscape. *Courtesy of Riverbend Pools*

This patio uses contrasting colors to mark paths and edges. Shelter from the summer elements can be found beyond the pool, in a tile-roofed pavilion with striking angular arches. *Courtesy of Paver Systems*

Pavilion

Above and left: A dining pavilion commands an excellent view of the surrounding patio. Inside, a wood-burning fireplace is the centerpiece of the room, separating the kitchenette from the dining area. *Courtesy of Gib-San Pools, Ltd.*

Planters and pool define the approach to a beautiful backyard pavilion. Atop this indoor/outdoor retreat, a decorative chimney rises, announcing the presence of a fireplace within. *Courtesy of Madison Swimming Pool Co., Inc.*

Gazebo

By definition, a gazebo is a garden structure with a view. Today these garden structures tend to take on an octagonal form, and ready-made gazebos sit awaiting a home in most landscape design yards. Generally, gazebos provide an intimate space where an individual, a romantic couple, or several friends might gather. Often a destination, whether placed at the end of a garden path, or the far reaches of a deck or patio, it affords a sense of intimacy and privacy to a small gathering. Its round shape creates a democratic forum where all are equal, and everyone is part of the conversation. Its angles also contribute to its usefulness as a focal point in the landscape, often highly decorated with Victorian-type scrollwork, elaborate railings, and a decorative cupola crown.

While homebuilders frequently ignore the façade of a home's rear view, a decorative gazebo is a quick solution in transforming it. This one, in white, keys in with the house while standing jewel-like atop a grey deck. *Courtesy of Casa Decks*

Situated off the main deck, a screened-in gazebo offers protection from occasional summer hazards like showers, mosquitoes, and other party-crashing insects. *Courtesy of Dream Decks*

Center left and left: A spacious deck and gazebo were constructed with contrasting white railings and a rich wood stain, providing a striking tie-in to the white house beyond. Wagon-spoke ornament in the gazebo windows contributes an element of privacy for those gathered within. *Courtesy of Dream Decks*

Vibrant Mediterranean red drapes cascade from this outdoor rotunda, adding color and sophistication, and the option of privacy to this romantic outdoor room. *Courtesy of Perennials Outdoor Fabrics*

Gazebo

Natural rocks form the columns of this stone gazebo that overlooks a vanishing edge pool. The surrounding landscape compliments the design of this neo-classical design. *Courtesy of Shasta Pools & Spas*

Planning and careful design make this small backyard space transform into a Japanese garden. A footbridge leads one to a wooden pagoda-like structure, a sheltered room under gull-winged roof. *Courtesy of St. Lawrence Pools Ltd.*

This patio is perfect for the family to enjoy outdoor activities. Among the amenities are swimming, boating, practice driving green, and an octagonal shelter where one can escape the sun. *Courtesy of EP Henry*

Two doors lead to two separate rooms in a pool house, his and hers for changing. *Courtesy of Gib-San Pools, Ltd.*

A pool house takes on the function of sculpture, adorning the far side of a sheltered pool area. *Courtesy of Gib-San Pools, Ltd.*

A pool house provides a sheltered, private space poolside. *Courtesy of Gib-San Pools, Ltd.*

Mimicking larger houses, a lot of pool houses are built with front or side porches. Porches like these offer a handy refuge in case of inclement weather or a place to store furniture so it is out of the way on the patio. *Courtesy of Gib-San Pools, Ltd.*

A pool house sports a long bar in front where drinks and food can be set out buffet style. *Courtesy of Gib-San Pools*

Mission roof tiles and yellow stucco give an outdoor room a distinctly Southwestern appearance. *Courtesy of Gib-San Pools, Ltd.*

The Pool House

True to our modest Victorian heritage, homeowners often opt to provide a pool house where guests might change into their swimsuits and back into clothing in privacy. They may house the pump and other workings of pool maintenance, and also provide off-season shelter to poolside furniture.

On the other hand, pool houses may also serve a very public role, acting as ringside theaters where all the activities of outdoor living can take place, from drink mixing to food preparation to sheltered dining centers. Some are even lushly appointed with living room-style furnishings where folks can make themselves comfortable. Others are equipped as guesthouse, so folks can stay as long as they like.

A pool house might take on any form, but is most often designed to mirror the home's architecture. Together with pool, patio, and other lawn structures, a landscape and home should work cohesively.

A small bathhouse forms part of the privacy barrier built along one side of this pool. *Courtesy of Gib-San, Ltd.*

A circular spa and bathhouse extend the home into the backyard. *Courtesy of Gib-San Pools, Ltd.*

Beside the waterfall, a slide waits to send swimmers shooting down and splashing into the pool. Slides like these usually have a tub hooked up to the water circulation system in the pool to keep the slides surface wet and slippery. *Courtesy of Gib-San Pools, Ltd.*

Placing the pool house at the far side of the pool acts as lure to draw people further into the yard. *Courtesy of Gib-San Pools, Ltd.*

While traditionally swimming pools have been rectangular or oval shaped, more contemporary pools have been dug in free-style shapes. *Courtesy of Gib-San Pools, Ltd.*

A restaurant-style eating bar juts out from the side of the pool house, safe from sun and rain under an overhang. Sliding glass doors part to reveal a living room set up inside. *Courtesy of Gib-San Pools, Ltd.*

Here a pool house has been painted blue with white trim and decorated with paddles and an anchor for a nautical theme. *Courtesy of Gib-San Pools, Ltd.*

Hot tub and pool are disguised as a clear-blue pond, with a rock garden "island" on one side, and a clean patio "beach" of imprinted concrete on the other. A pavilion creates a shady place to gather and socialize. *Courtesy of Bomanite Corporation*

On the edge of the woods sits a quaint bathhouse, complete with covered grill and lounge area in front of a fireplace. *Courtesy of Artistic Pools, Inc.*

A pool house gives shade seekers a place to lounge. Family and guests can sit at a sheltered table for meals and refreshments served from a kitchen within. *Courtesy of Madison Swimming Pool Co., Inc.*

A shining pool house stands above this free form pool. Underwater magic is achieved with blue lighting. *Courtesy of Gym & Swim*

A corner pool house at the far side of the pool lures home occupants far from their daily cares. *Courtesy of Prestige Pools & Spas, Inc.*

A small pool house is big on architecture, with a rounded dormer window and plenty of panes to illuminate the interior. *Courtesy of Gib-San Pools, Ltd.*

A pool house has been dedicated to providing a protected area for outdoor revels, with a small changing room for privacy. *Courtesy of Memphis Pool Supply Co.*

A pool house provides shelter, changing rooms, and, most importantly, a mini bar. *Courtesy of Gib-San Pools, Ltd.*

Glass-paneled doors draw open to create an inviting entrance to this pool house. *Courtesy of Gym & Swim*

A handsome pool house overlooks black reflecting pool and spa. Water spills out from a small chute in the spa and then in turn spills over the vanishing edge of the pool. *Courtesy of Artistic Pools*

A pent roof provides additional shade and shelter for the entryway to this pool house. *Courtesy of Gym & Swim*

Pyramid shapes are reflected around the pool, most notably in the two spires of a conservatory/pool house roof. *Courtesy of Oslund and Associates*

The little watering hole next to the larger one has whimsically been called McTiki. *Courtesy of Maryland Pools, Inc.*

A pool house offers sheltered seating where one can belly up to the bar. *Courtesy of Gym & Swim*

A gatehouse-like structure is reflected in the rectangular pool. Under a covered porch sit a table and chairs. *Courtesy of Madison Swimming Pool Co., Inc.*

A pool house forms the focal point at the far end of the pool. *Courtesy of Gym & Swim*

A widow's walk effect tops the pool house, creating a classic shore-style profile. *Courtesy of Rizzo Pool Construction Co.*

A wooden trellis coming out from the kitchen creates a united outdoor space. The enclosed kitchen creates a space where the cook can work without being disturbed by the weather or guests. Everyone got their space on this patio, including an avid golfer who got his putting green. *Courtesy of Gib-San Pools, Ltd.*

Arches and columns add classic appeal to this impressive pool house. *Courtesy of Harrison Design Associates*

An extensive backyard landscape includes expansive patio pool, spa, and an enviable pool house. *Courtesy of Gym & Swim*

These homeowners indulged in pure whimsy when decorating their pool house. You wouldn't know it from the classic architecture of the façade, but inside is quite another story! *Courtesy of Harrison Design Associates*

Covered
Passageways

A brick colonnade functions as sheltered passageway, but is spacious enough to double as a patio for those who want to linger. *Courtesy of Telescope Casual Furniture, Inc.*

A latticed roofline creates a framework for indoor/outdoor gatherings between two outdoor structures. *Courtesy of David Gast & Associates*

Left: This hot tub has been built for entertaining, large enough to accommodate a dozen in a pinch. Beyond, an arched colonnade provides shade and shelter. *Courtesy of Artistic Pools*

Temporary Structures

If variety is the spice of life, temporary structures for the yard add seasoning. After all, it doesn't make sense to build a 2,000-square foot pavilion to marry off your only daughter. That's what rentals are for. Moreover, in four-season regions, you're only going to use the yard a small percentage of the time. Shelter that you can pack up and put away makes sense. You save money by buying smaller, and you save your investment by putting it away when not in use.

Also, lightweight and portable structures allow you to be much more creative in your landscape arrangements. An umbrella can be rotated with the sun. A canvas gazebo can emerge for a special weekend.

Gauzy curtains draw back to reveal an outdoor alcove. Because white reflects light and is less likely to bleach or fade in the sun, it is frequently used for outdoor furniture and decoration. *Courtesy of Harrison Design Associates*

Right: A few simple knots and curtains can be drawn or opened to connect this patio space with the beautiful gardens, or closet it away for a little tête-à-tête. Dark brown furniture contrasts nicely with the yellow curtains and flagstone floors. *Courtesy of Brown Jordan*

A metal-framed gazebo creates a varied room for a walled patio space, allowing the curtains to be drawn or thrown wide depending on the weather or temperament. *Courtesy of Susan Cohen Associates, Inc.*

Light gauzy curtains give this backyard pavilion a delicate and airy appearance. The curtains offer an option of privacy or connection as the mood may suit. *Courtesy of Dan Berger, LandPlan Landscaping*

Frequently found in parks and other public places, gazeboes fit equally as well in private spaces like backyards and gardens. Here a gazebo becomes a backyard retreat furnished with curling cast iron furniture. The curtains can be adjusted for privacy or shade. *Courtesy of Laneventure*

An umbrella, raised, creates its own micro-climate, shielding occupants from harsh rays and prying eyes on this intimate patio space.

A stylish wicker dining set provides contrast to the light, contemporary design of the patio and custom barbeque grill. *Courtesy of Park Slope Design*

Here the patio furniture, the eating bar, and the barbeque have all been colored to complement the dusty rose color of the patio. *Courtesy of Custom Pools, Inc.*

Canvas sheets are a stylish solution to the desert's lack of shade trees. Their flat surfaces keep an open view to the surrounding gardens, while allowing breezes full access to the occupants. Stucco walls segregate sections of the patio without interfering with the overall open feeling. *Courtesy of Dan Berger, LandPlan Landscaping*

Left: A portable gazebo shelters a casual dining set, creating a poolside oasis. *Courtesy of Tropitone*

Elements That Create a "Room"

A half stone wall with a built-in stacked stone water feature encircles this corner stone courtyard. *Courtesy of Park Slope Design.*

The whole point of being outside isn't to be "in" a room. However, there are times when the great outdoors is more enjoyable when broken into "room-like" spaces. A certain comfort level can be obtained by carving out an area conducive to conversation, digestion, or simple relaxation. Humans tend to congregate in carefully defined places, and the backyard is no exception. Though this entire book is dedicated to the idea of outdoor rooms, this chapter, in particular, draws attention to smaller, non-architectural details that help make us feel "at home" outdoors.

Walls

Whether a half wall that affords seating or a tall wall that intentionally obscures the view, mankind has been creating solid barriers outdoors for as long as anyone has called themselves a "landscape designer."

Large paver stones were set to allow channels of greenery on the floor of this semi-formal outdoor room. The stucco wall and arch further enhance the Spanish style design. *Courtesy of Park Slope Design*

Vines climb up the pillars supporting a lattice-work trellis. Beneath the trellis, a wicker table and chairs stand ready for any kind of meal, ranging from a simple midmorning snack to an elaborate evening dinner. The furniture and the surroundings recall elegant dining in far off places like Spain or Italy. *Courtesy of Winston Furniture*

Limited lawn space around a full-size pool was expanded to allow a container garden to flourish on a vertical surface. The stucco and wood wall is adorned with a sculpted sheet of copper, which provides lustrous depth to the narrow space. *Courtesy of Dan Berger, Land-Plan Landscaping*

A mix of attractive materials – flagstones, pebbles, metal , wicker, and stucco create a visual medley in this small Spanish courtyard. *Courtesy of Park Slope Design*

Salvage Stars

Local salvage yards are one way of gleaning unique items to set your outdoor spaces apart. For instance, old columns and fencing can be had, and already come with the patina of age that adds charm to a garden.

A carved antique wooden headboard adds an interesting decorative element to an outdoor patio. *Courtesy of Harrison Design Associates*

Stacked riverstone makes a handsome wall for this patio dining area. *Courtesy of O.W. Lee, Inc.*

A retaining wall provides bench seating, and adds intimacy to an outdoor dining space furnished with teak. *Courtesy of Barlow Tyrie*

Ceramic tiles set in a sunburst pattern decorate the top of this table. *Courtesy of O.W. Lee, Inc.*

Above: An ornamental garden centers around a birdbath, set against an impressive backdrop of fence-topped wall. *Courtesy of Environmental Landscape Associates, Inc.*

Bottom left: A vine-covered arbor provides refreshing shade for a patio. Between the arbor's shade above and the cool stone tiles on the floor, this patio provides an excellent retreat on a hot summer's day. *Courtesy of Winston Furniture*

Shaded by trees and secluded by a brick wall, a random stone patio offers a restful retreat from the hectic pace of the everyday household. Here people can gather, enjoy the fresh air, and take a break from everyday activities and concerns. *Courtesy of Brown Jordan*

Patio furniture lounges around the edge of a small swimming pool. The blue upholstery of the furniture compliments the water and tiles of the pools. High bricks walls bring a sense of privacy to this relaxing environment. *Courtesy of Brown Jordan*

A fork in the garden path branches off into a secluded spot ringed with trees and bushes, and is defined by a half wall set bench height.

Half walls define a patio space, and add seating as well as display options. *Courtesy of Unilock*

A semi-circle of retaining wall acts as seating, or simply defines a cozy nook on a paver patio. *Courtesy of Oaks Concrete Products*

Sometimes the person you are designing for is the household's smallest. A small retaining wall contains a sand play area, and a brick doorway opens on the imagination. *Courtesy of Jon Larson, Jarvis Architects*

Decorative Railings & Fences

Ironwork and wood are natural compliments to a garden setting, and create stunning effects when used to define space outdoors. A safety factor in defining steep drop-offs, railings need not be limited to the sharp edges. The introduction of a railing can create a whole new space within the backyard setting.

An elevated platform commands a view of the yard, emphasized by the power hue of red in cushions and accents. The room's distance from the house indicates that it is intended to be a "private" outdoor room where a person can relax or entertain visitors without fear of disruption or distraction. *Courtesy of Winston Furniture*

Ivy lends an air of antiquity and dignity to this outdoor room, defined by walls with inset cast-iron grates to open the view for those who are seated. *Courtesy of Winston Furniture*

Decorative Railings & Fences

Potted Walls

For the same effect as a half wall, arrange evenly spaced planters, fill with decorative grasses, water, and enjoy. Likewise, you can create a corner simply by massing planters of the same or varying heights into an el formation.

The decorative railing encircles a raised patio, where low-lying chairs and thick cushions invite homeowners and their friends to sit a spell. *Courtesy of Gloster Furniture, Inc.*

A decorative rail emphasizes the attention paid to detail in the design of this patio space. *Courtesy of Harrison Design Associates*

Half-inch thick tempered glazing poured over aluminum mesh on the floor and the same type of glazing, molded into a railing compliment this beachfront home's modern look nicely. The blue color and glassy appearance of the deck's floor is reminiscent of the ocean that sits a few feet from the house. *Courtesy of David Lawrence Gray Architects*

Iron balusters have been curved to give the deck a decorative element. *Courtesy of Deckorators, Inc.*

Wood and iron team up to frame a spectacular mountain view. *Courtesy of Deckorators, Inc.*

Raised Beds

Retaining walls can be installed and filled to create raised planters. Not only do these help vary the site lines within a flat topography, they offer a place to sit within the landscape.

Left: Wrought iron curves add a little decorative touch to these balusters. *Courtesy of Deckorators, Inc.*

A curved railing follows the contours of the deck beneath it. *Courtesy of Deckorators, Inc.*

Decorative torches cap railing posts for night lighting and daytime awe. *Courtesy of Deckorators, Inc.*

A corner bench provides architecture, a sense of shelter, and an alluring cozy place for intimate gatherings along the lattice railing of this expansive deck. *Courtesy of the California Redwood Association*

Geometric cutouts form an intricate decorative pattern, commonly referred to as Chinese Chippendale. *Courtesy of the California Redwood Association*

Decorative Railings & Fences

Top left: A redwood planter was wired for electric lighting. *Courtesy of the California Redwood Association*

Center: An arched entryway fitted with a fanciful wrought iron gate acts as ornament to its patio setting. *Courtesy of Dan Berger, LandPlan Landscaping*

An umbrella creates the illusion of ceiling, while a lattice fence with scalloped top-line provides a decorative "wall." The effect is a patio room, without the closed-in feeling. *Courtesy of Barlow Tyrie*

A decorative fence and gate create awe for this portal to an outdoor room.
Courtesy of Environmental Landscape Associates, Inc.

A stone bench, open railing, and a tangle of wisteria vine combine for a primitive retreat space.
Courtesy of Brian Higley, Landscape Architect

Decorative Railings & Fences

Above and top right: A redwood deck features an overhead shade shelter, a spa, and a built-in conversation pit. An artful fence provides a decorative backdrop. *Courtesy of the California Redwood Association*

Dark wicker adds a stylish, sophisticated touch to this patio setting, accented with a flashy red textile. Wrought iron and a carefully trimmed hedge form a half wall. *Courtesy of Brown Jordan*

Above: Outdoor furniture stands in for an entire living room suite, formal in fashion, and cushioned for comfort. *Courtesy of Brown Jordan*

Right: Flagstones were upended to form a raised flowerbed, in complement to the surrounding patio surface. *Courtesy of Dan Berger, LandPlan Landscaping*

Decorative Railings & Fences

Above: Hedges and short walls were used to create nooks and crannies in this patio's setting. *Courtesy of Brown Jordan*

Top right: There's room for a whole army within this yard bordered by latticework and stone. Within this game spot, a concrete and tile pad invites the competitive to engage in The Sport of Kings. *Courtesy of Peter A. Zepponi*

Fiberglass walls and a wooden stage area were married for a semi-private space in a great open lawn, designed by Dean Cardasis Associates, Brian Higley, Christine Brestrup, and Christ Baxter, for a garden in Massachusetts. When not in use for public events, the intriguing effect of the space invariably draws people to explore the perimeters. *Courtesy of Brian Higley, Landscape Architect / Architecture by Peter Sweeny, Architect*

Surface Materials

A statue points out our basic needs, Nature provides bounteous amenities, we need only to insert ourselves to enjoy them. *Courtesy of Brian Higley, Landscape Architect*

Whatever material you choose to serve underfoot in your outdoor rooms, the goal at the end of the day is to enjoy it. If your area tends to be damp, you'll find the backyard more accessible with hardscaped paths and raised patios. If you live in a dryer climate, Nature itself might serve adequately for frequent escapes. If you entertain often, you'll need to provide safe, level surfaces that allow hordes of feet to tramp without trampling delicate lawn or plantings. Once your needs are established, an endless variety of materials awaits your decision, from wood decking to decorative concrete, pavers, and stones.

The Lawn

So simple, so desirable, such an inherent part of suburban life, the green grass bed that we slave over every weekend need not be just for show. Grass is a wonderful, inviting surface often neglected in the enjoyment department. To more fully utilize your lawn, try luring yourself out with inviting furniture and cool refreshments on a sunny day.

Lightweight aluminum furniture allows for impromptu lawn gatherings.
Courtesy of Brown Jordan

A series of small inclines and circles creates a three-tiered garden. Flagstone rings separate the flowers from the grass, making it look like the lawn has flowed down the steps and collected in pools. *Courtesy of Environmental Landscape Associates, Inc.*

Lightweight aluminum furniture allows picnickers the possibility of outsmarting the ants.
Courtesy of Telescope Casual Furniture, Inc.

Pavestones invite a contemplative stroll to a sitting area in this small urban yard.
Courtesy of Park Slope Design

Top Left: Asian influences in outdoor furnishings are visible in seating with deep-cushioned comfort. *Courtesy of Sutherland and Perennials Outdoor Fabrics*

Top Right: A permanent structure offers lawn seating while taking up a minimal footprint in the yard. Fanciful colors on the beaded pillar and gingerbread-adorned roof make it function equally as lawn decoration and seating.

Stepping stones soften the transition from concrete to lawn. A lap lane/reflecting pool divides the space, creating a more gentle flow of foot traffic. *Courtesy of Oslund and Associates*

Rock facing on the home was matched for the retaining wall that supports this raised redwood deck. The result is a continuation of the architecture into the lawn. *Courtesy of the California Redwood Association*

Decks

Long a staple of outdoor expansion, decks are no longer just wood structures. Today's homeowner has a choice in decking material ranging from different varieties and grades of wood to recycled plastics and vinyl. The newer materials are often far easier in terms of maintenance, and offer endless variety in terms of color. However, there are those that still swear by wood for its natural beauty.

A deck nestled amidst a thicket of bamboo and palm provides a retreat. Red upholstery creates an interesting visual statement. *Courtesy of Carter Grandle*

This multi-level deck interconnects and ushers you to different water features including a water fountain, waterfall, and hot tub. *Courtesy of Gym & Swim*

A built-in counter and cabinetry, plumbed with a sink, provides space for food preparation and buffet service on this satellite deck. *Courtesy of the California Redwood Association*

Concrete has been cast and stained to create a beautiful mosaic floor within a substantial loggia. *Courtesy of XcelDeck*™

Patios

Concrete

Not your plain old slab anymore, installers now specialize in stamped, stenciled, and stained concrete applications that can recreate almost any surface or design imaginable. From wildly colorful to dead-on imitations of natural stone or fossilized rocks, concrete can be custom poured for a look unique to your home and lifestyle.

Radiating waves provide a natural progression of hardscape connecting the home to the lawn beyond. The effect was created using two different finishing techniques on a concrete slab. *Courtesy of Dan Berger, LandPlan Landscaping*

Top left: Concrete was carefully stained using finishing powders and stencils for an amazing imitation of flagstone. Sling-back chairs add the perfect accent to a patio encircled by tropical lush. *Courtesy of Tropitone*

Top right: A jigsaw flagstone effect was created for this stucco walled porch, hunkered beneath wooden beams in a setting inspired by the down to earth architecture of Mexico and the Southwestern United States. A woven blanket and a pair of flowerpots add a splash of color to the earth-toned décor. *Courtesy of Jim Hayes*

Pigmented powders actually harden the concrete surface, as well as provide a mottled surface that accurately mimics natural stone. Open on all sides, this lanai affords elevated views of the surrounding garden. *Courtesy of O.W. Lee, Inc.*

Right: Matching retaining wall material and paver stones were married for this cascading patio. A border stone helps to define the edges and create variety. *Courtesy of Belgard-Permacon*

Pavers

The greatest revolution taking place in the backyard today is the increasing variety and availability of concrete pavers. Once limited to natural stone, clay bricks, or poured concrete when considering a patio, today's homeowner can select from a vast array of pavers. Coloring and finishing techniques create pavers that accurately imitate bricks, from the crisp corners of brand new to tumbled edges that mimic aging. Likewise, concrete can accurately recreate stone, cobblestone, keystone, and any imaginable shape and color. A visit to a landscaping yard is an exciting eye-opener.

Special saws can cut pavers to create custom designs such as this one, done in two tones for dramatic effect. The resulting paver mosaic forms a focal point for a dining set. Red buds and palm trees form the backdrop for this tropical outdoor room. *Courtesy of Carter Grandle*

Patios

Radiating pavers form a perfect circular patio, and a destination close by the water's edge. *Courtesy of Ideal Concrete Block Company, Inc.*

Bottom left: A running brick pattern circles this patio, a classic design enjoyed for centuries in landscape design. Bistro-style bar stools and table make much of the petite space. *Courtesy of American Home Furnishings Alliance*

Bottom right: The same brick pattern is shown in a different earth tone. A set of stairs leads down to this intimate brick patio, where cast-iron patio chairs shelter beneath an umbrella. *Courtesy of Brown Jordan*

Pavers are laid on a carefully prepared bed of gravel and sand, the cracks between them filled with more sand. When done properly, they can withstand years of use. Improperly laid, or subjected to considerable ground shifts, they are relatively easy to pick up and reinstall. Likewise, they can be reused and reconfigured should the homeowner's needs change. This patio may be modest in size, but it has all the amenities: fireplace, cook center, and a variety of comfortable seating options. *Courtesy of Mutual Materials Co.*

Bottom left: A variety of plants and trees surround this small patio, creating a small private space in the greater area outside the house. *Courtesy of Brown Jordan*

Bottom right: Here metal patio furniture has been coated with weatherproof finish and painted a bronze color to compliment the patio pavers. *Courtesy of Laneventure*

Mixing it Up

Add variety and visual interest by mixing and matching different paving materials within your landscape. By creating different surfaces, you add destinations, and a sense of purposeful zoning to your backyard spaces.

Pea gravel and concrete block were combined to provide cleared spaces within the landscape. Teak furnishings provide the comforts of home outdoors. A teak ice chest keeps soda and wine cold in the warm summer sun. When the weather gets too cold, the chairs and the other furniture can be folded up and stored away until "patio season" returns. *Courtesy of Barlow Tyrie*

Bottom left: Levels of decking, concrete, wood, and lawn create contemporary elegance in this outdoor living space. *Courtesy of Brown Jordan*

Bottom right: Grass defines spaces within a flagstone patio, creating seating areas and cooking space. *Courtesy of O.W. Lee, Inc.*

A primitive stone bench in a small patch of pea-gravel provide basics for a contemplative moment in nature. *Courtesy of Brian Higley, Landscape Architect*

Garden walls frame the borrowed view beyond the granite pool deck – offering a glimpse of the serene. Polished concrete and loose pea gravel stand in stark contrast for a contemporary landscape scene. *Courtesy of Oslund and Associates*

An intimate circle of hardscaping stands amidst lawn and loose stone, where a ceramic pot bubbles over with the most subtle of fountain music.

A step from the deck, a sunken, circular area becomes a natural point where folks settle. A swing, just off to the side, offers alternative seating. *Courtesy of Jon Larson, Jarvis Architects*

A corner spa, framed by two stretches of wood trellis, creates a focal point at the far side of a natural stone patio. Potted plants set on steps help the spa blend in with its exquisitely natural surroundings. *Courtesy of Dan Berger, LandPlan Landscaping*

Plantings soften a flagstone patio, flanked by half walls, which offer year-round seating. *Courtesy of Julia Fogg, Landscape Architect*

The Four Elements

Air is the main reason we feel compelled to move outdoors. There it is considered fresher, whether cleaner than the stale air trapped within four walls, or simply circulating more freely, it is invigorating to be in the open air. Earth, too, is the given element of outdoor living. Here we are closer to the soil and its fruits, our feet firmly planted upon solid ground. To complete the picture, landscape designers often add the two missing elements that make up the foursome the ancients associated with life – fire and water. These two pieces of the picture offer a timeless, primal appeal, as you'll see in the following illustrations.

Air, earth, fire, and water all play a role in an inviting outdoor environment. A growing trend in pool design is the effect of a natural body of water. Here it would seem that waterfalls flow from a natural spring. After swimming in the pool, bathers can get out and dry of in front of the fireplace just beyond. *Courtesy of MarcoDesigns*

A fireplace dominates a raised semi-circle, overlooking a pool that mimics nature in its random shape, and the spring-like cascade of water. *Courtesy of Artistic Pools*

Water, fire, earth, and air are all combined in a backyard paradise. A lit waterfall across blue tiles is an aural and visual focal point. A partially shaded table and chairs close to the grill await family and guests. *Courtesy of Bill Dial and Sterling Landscape*

A small fountain burbles, center stage in a patio setting. The movement of water, like the licking of flames, offers a meditative focal point, soothing and absorbing for those who find the time to enjoy it.

A spa doubles as water fountain in this backyard environment, its shape mirrored in the background by a circular firepit. *Courtesy of Moss Landscaping*

Unique furnishings, from Adirondack chairs with a twist, to a lemony pop-up umbrella, add an aura of fun to a splashing, lily pond retreat. *Courtesy of Santa Barbara Designs*

Top left: A stone grotto tucked under a deck creates a cool and alluring retreat in the heat of the summer. Bench seating around a roaring waterfall proves irresistible. *Courtesy of Harrison Design*

Top right: A patinaed copper fountain at the edge of this fireplace-studded patio adds an earthy sensibility to a modernist style retreat. *Courtesy of Michael McCarthy, Shipley ArchitectsAssociates*

Water trickles down the sides of a bronze urn situated in the middle of a fountain. *Courtesy of Montana Ave. Interiors*

Dining Al Fresco

Eating outdoors has universal appeal, whether one has time to pack a picnic and head to a beautiful park, or simply to take the meal on a balcony. Today's homeowners yearn for that special place just beyond the kitchen, where the family can gather in the fresh air for refreshments. Special occasions aside, the goal is to make the outdoor spaces as convenient and maintenance free as possible. And to spend as much time as possible out there. Toward this end, many backyards now include grilling stations, drink bars, and in the best of all worlds, their own outdoor kitchens.

Comfortable chairs and a big dining table allow this family to linger outdoors, and a retractable canvas awning helps to control nature's influence on the patio environment. *Courtesy of Susan Cohen Associates, Inc.*

Left: Teak wood possesses naturally occurring oils that make it extremely weather resistant, even if it is not treated with varnish or sealant. Thus it is highly sought after for outdoor furniture. Here it was used to make a large banquet-style table, folding chairs, and an outdoor sideboard. *Courtesy of Barlow Tyrie*

Garden areas and container plants create a tropical atmosphere in this courtyard environment. *Courtesy of O.W. Lee, Inc.*

Far left: An arbor covered with blooming flowers forms a breathtaking background for this dining area. *Courtesy of Brown Jordan*

Beautifully carved pillars support a thatched roof over a dining room patio. Beyond the patio, a hedge of bamboo rings an outdoor pool and spa. *Courtesy of Susan Cohen Associates, Inc.*

Yellow walls and pillars were topped with a pergola to provide shade and a sense of security to outdoor dinner guests. A bar wraps around the grill center to give the cook a designated work zone and to provide him with some company, too. *Courtesy of Kelly Melendez, MAK Studio*

Foliage embraces this patio in a thicket of classical greenery – a mosaic table and thick cushioned chairs serving as centerpiece. *Courtesy of O.W. Lee, Inc.*

Left: A dining table has been sunk into the ground and a sandstone patio built up around it. Guests sit crosslegged on small flagstones or dangle their legs down into the hole surrounding the table. Dining here offers an interesting experience that brings diners down to eye level with the foliage. *Courtesy of Dan Berger, LandPlan Landscaping*

Far left: A southwest feel is created through color and texture for this outdoor dining area.

Bar-side Seating

Whether wet or muddy from gardening, or simply surrounded by friends, it's annoying to have to head indoors even for refreshments. So lots of landscape designers are making allowances for that little bar refrigerator, a sink, and other amenities to be housed right on the patio. Belly up and enjoy!

Outdoor stools circle a granite bar in this poolside environment. *Courtesy of O.W. Lee, Inc.*

A wooden trellis links the outdoor kitchen with a garden area. *Courtesy of Gib-San Pools, Ltd.*

A hanging umbrella helps shade the grill area without a cumbersome pole getting in the way of the cook. *Courtesy of Gib-San Pools, Ltd.*

Bar-side Seating

Right: An outdoor kitchen is sheltered underneath the covered patio of a Southwestern style home. The space beyond the kitchen opens up into a courtyard with a swimming pool. *Courtesy of Toll Brothers*

Far right: An archway opening in the brick wall of this pool house forms a welcome invitation for sun bathers in need of refreshment. *Courtesy of Greenville Pool & Supply Co.*

Here's an outdoor room furnished for entertaining, complete with plenty of room and seating for guests, a table for sit-down meals, and a bar for making and serving drinks and light snacks. *Courtesy of McGarvey Custom Homes*

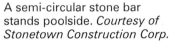

A semi-circular stone bar stands poolside. *Courtesy of Stonetown Construction Corp.*

Seating need only offer oxygen to the upper reaches of the body. Here those indulging in a visit to the bar needn't leave the pool. *Courtesy of Maryland Pools, Inc.*

A mobile eating bar is a handy thing to have for entertaining – it can be moved closer to the kitchen so dishes don't have so far to travel, or tucked in a corner to keep it out of the way. *Courtesy of O.W. Lee, Inc.*

Bar-side Seating

Three bar sections stand alone or united, a clever innovation in patio furniture that brings convenience, and service, into the open air, and tucks them away off season. *Courtesy of O.W. Lee. Inc.*

Wicker's versatility and tropical appeal are demonstrated in an outdoor area/barroom. *Courtesy of Gloster Furniture, Inc.*

Below: A portable drink cart and bar can double as a buffet during large gatherings. *Courtesy of O.W. Lee, Inc.*

An example of the increasingly sophisticated grills available to homeowners today. Here a chef can grill on the main range or use rotisserie attachments. A shelf above keeps other dishes warm until it's time for them to be served. A cabinet beneath the range houses the propane tank and a small refrigerator for drinks and dishes that need to be kept cold. The doors themselves have hooks for grilling tools and shelves for sauces and condiments. *Courtesy of Empire Comfort Systems, Inc.*

Grill Thrills

An entire male-dominated subculture has grown up around the grill. Evolved from the campfire cooking of our ancestors, today's grills have refined and sanitized outdoor cooking while preserving the charcoal and smoke flavors that excite our senses. Grill centers have long been a staple of outdoor design, whether portable units or lovingly constructed brick centers. Today they are becoming increasingly sophisticated.

Intended for some heavy-duty outdoor cooking, this barbeque comes with an extra-wide grill and a gas burner set low to enable chefs to more easily tend large steamers and high-capacity pots. *Courtesy of Robert H. Peterson Co. and Fire Magic*

Besides a grill and a gas burner, this barbeque station also includes a warming tray to keep buns warm and a refrigerator to keep condiments cold and greens fresh. *Courtesy of Robert H. Peterson Co. and Fire Magic*

A barbeque center is conveniently located next to the back door, set within a stone wall complete with buffet shelf perfect for outdoor serving. *Courtesy of Conte & Conte, LLC*

Below: A barbeque and eating bar has been situated halfway between the pool and a pavilion, convenient to both outdoor gathering places. Umbrellas can be fitted onto the counter of the eating bar to help keep the sun off the people sitting there. *Courtesy of Custom Pools, Inc.*

An outdoor grill shelters under the overhang of this house. The counter is equipped with stainless steel cabinets for holding grilling tools and the propane tank. A stainless steel sink means that utensils can be washed outside instead of having to be taken inside. *Courtesy of Brick SouthEast, Inc.*

Below: An outdoor kitchen is equipped for the perfect weekend barbeque. The grill comes with a warming shelf and can be fitted with a spit for roasting. The island comes with refrigerator, a single side burner for cooking sauces and side dishes, four drawers for keeping utensils, and an open cooler for keeping drinks cold and at hand. *Courtesy of Laneventure*

Top left: A stone counter houses a pair of barbeque grills, perfect for large parties and for grilling a wide selection of food items. *Courtesy of Buechel Stone Corp.*

Top right: Brick defines the refreshment area that includes a fridge, tap, and grill to serve family and friends. *Courtesy of Gym & Swim*

A corner barbecue station also offers bar-side seating, allowing the chef to work center stage, and guests to sample tidbits fresh from the fire. *Courtesy of Custom Pools, Inc.*

For barbeques and other outdoor meals, an outdoor eating bar easily accommodates a crowd. *Courtesy of Environmental Landscape Associates, Inc.*

Photo © LOF Productions

Instead of brick or stone, this outdoor barbeque was sheathed in wooden shingles. Very popular in New England, Shingle Style architecture became popular in American architecture and design after 1876. *Courtesy of Fryday & Doyne Architecture Interior Design*

Sculptural elements like the elephant-raised planter, the chair armrests, and the wrought-iron table support, give this open-air room its rarified air. *Courtesy of The Uncommon Designer*

Left: A riverstone-clad barbeque borders the marina. Counter space on either side of the grill can be used while cooking or as a buffet table when the meal is ready. *Courtesy of TimberTech*

A stone barbeque transforms this patio into a secluded alcove just the right size for family gatherings and special meals. *Courtesy of Toll Brothers*

Below: A tile-backed cook station is perfect for a tropical climate, where grouting doesn't have to stand the test of freeze and thaw. *Courtesy of Telescope Casual Furniture, Inc.*

A backyard pavilion was fashioned to function as a dream kitchen for an avid grill chef. Fencing provides privacy walls for the suburban setting, where friends and family frequently gather to enjoy company, fresh air, and the fruits of the owner's culinary labor. *Courtesy of Remodeling Services*

Iron Woods cabinetry and counters provide a handsome deck addition, made all the more attractive by their centerpiece – a barbeque unit. *Courtesy of Cecco Trading, Inc.*

Center right and bottom right: An arbor shades sections of this patio, where a waterfall and goldfish pond add tranquility and beauty to the space. A barbecue station is a central gathering point from which to enjoy the surroundings. *Courtesy of Dan Berger, LandPlan Landscaping*

Wood-fired Ovens

An increasingly popular outdoor installation is the wood-fired oven, a small fireplace that is super heated with kindling, then the fire is swept aside and pizzas and breads are prepared within minutes. This age-old, simple technology has entire cults dedicated to its perfection, from the perfect shape of the interior, to the perfect make-up of the oven material. An imperfect science, wood ovens lend themselves to fun and scrumptious culinary experimentation.

A fire heats a wood oven while pizzas lie at the ready. A mop-like tool will be used to sweep the fire and ash aside once the oven is hot enough to quick-cook the food. This sculpted oven has been decorated with a grape leaf motif to enhance its Mediterranean appearance. *Courtesy of Alchymia Wood Fired Ovens*

Below: A party-sized grill shares top billing with a wood-fired oven and an open hearth is this three-part fireside special. *Courtesy of Conte & Conte, LLC*

Wood-fired ovens can be built in various sizes and forms. A round oven like this one heats up fairly quickly and evenly, which makes it ideally suited for cooking pizza *Courtesy of Fogazzo Wood Fired Ovens and Barbeques*

A peaked roof and a concrete chimney make this oven look like a little house. To match the surrounding countertops this wood-fired oven was fitted with luminous granite tiles around the oven door opening. *Courtesy of Fogazzo Wood Fired Ovens and Barbeques*

Entire Kitchens Outdoors

For the family that has it all, there's more to be had. Particularly in warm climates, the outdoor kitchen is becoming an essential ingredient of home design. From refrigeration, to cook units, to running water, storage space, and countertop, what used to be the domain of indoors is moving out.

Not for the casual outdoor cook, this outdoor kitchen is equipped with a grill, a range, and a wood-fired oven. *Courtesy of Karen Black's Kitchens and Rooms by Design*

A sheltered porch houses a complete kitchen including granite countertops and custom cabinets. The ceiling as well as bead-board backsplash and island provide additional texture and interest. *Courtesy of Haynes Associates*

An outdoor kitchen centered around a conical wood-fired oven celebrates Italian cuisine. The kitchen area has wooden roof with skylights, allowing its use throughout Northern Californian year. *Courtesy of H. Davis Construction Company*

Entire Kitchens Outdoors

The area between two wings of a house becomes prime space for an outdoor kitchen. A wood-fired oven, a range, a prep sink, and a refrigerator mean this kitchen is equipped for any occasion from a breakfast for one to a weekend barbeque. A TV situated near the ceiling is visible from both the kitchen and the eating bar. *Courtesy of Fogozzo Wood Fired Ovens and Barbeques*

A large palm tree, two umbrellas, and a section of overhang help shade sections of this patio, equipped with a kitchen. *Courtesy of MarcoDesigns*

Wooden latticework encloses this outdoor kitchen, giving the space a comfortable sense of privacy without disrupting the flow inherent in "open air." Features include a wood-fired oven, stainless steel storage cabinets, two side range worktop burners, an under counter refrigerator, a prep sink, and a barbeque grill. *Courtesy of Peter A. Zepponi*

A loggia becomes an everyday room in temperate weather. Here a complete kitchen, dining area, and living room furnish the family's daily communal needs. *Courtesy of Peter A. Zepponi*

Left: An outdoor kitchen like this one allows the cook to be part of outdoor activities, while the tools of his or her trade stay sheltered. *Courtesy of Moss Landscaping*

Courtesy of McGarvey Custom Homes

Whitewashed bricks compliment the slate flagstones on the patio. Within these natural elements, the latest in stainless steel appliances afford modern convenience. *Courtesy of Laneventure*

A checkered backsplash and stone hood draw attention to the rear of this poolside kitchen. *Courtesy of Harbourside Custom Homes*

Nothing is set in stone, except for this kitchen that is. Half walls define this outdoor kitchen, where the fire pit, eating bar, and all the counters were all crafted from stone. A stainless steel range and sink complement the gray tone of the countertops. *Courtesy of Classic Garden Design LLC*

An entire kitchen has been moved out of doors. Features like an electric oven, gas range, and industrial-strength hood stand ready to serve picnickers. A brick tile eating counter reproduces an interior pattern with durable outdoor materials. *Courtesy of Karen Black's Kitchens and Rooms by Design*

Concrete applications are becoming increasingly versatile, and craftsmen more accomplished. In this case, stone walls are actually molded and stained from concrete coatings, and the countertop is cast concrete carefully finished for a nearly impermeable surface ideally suited to outdoor kitchens. *Courtesy of The Concrete Impressionist*

Below: Backyards and grills are natural go-togethers. This elaborate stone cook center is every epicure's dream. Set within an expansive pavilion, it's practically weatherproof, eliminating the need for "rain dates" on the invitations. *Courtesy of Karen Black's Kitchens and Rooms by Design*

A wooden trellis and glass-paneled doors define a space, while falling shy of isolating it from the greater outdoors. A complete kitchen, a dining area, and a "living room" fitted with a fireplace, provide for total outdoor living. *Courtesy of Dan Berger, LandPlan Landscaping*

A two-stage waterfall adds park-like atmosphere to an outdoor cook station, providing a small bench for waterfront seating, and cool counterpart to the hot work of grilling. *Courtesy of Inside Out*

Left: A stainless steel range and a wood-fired oven eagerly await the next backyard barbeque. The patio is open with plenty of room for barbeque guests to meet and mingle. Away from the grill and the oven, a statue of a bear dangles his toes over a lily pond and keeps his eyes wide open for goldfish. *Courtesy of Dan Berger, LandPlan Landscaping*

The area around this pool has been transformed into the ultimate backyard retreat with features like a spa and a raised dining area complete with a barbeque and food prep area. Variations in the paving and scattered flowerbeds add color and visual interest to the area. *Courtesy of Pool Tech Midwest Inc.*

A kitchen opens to the treetops, for *al fresco* dining and cooking. *Courtesy of Gym & Swim*

Bottom left and right: A complete kitchen area is sheltered by a shingle roof, making it all-weather ready for poolside entertaining. *Courtesy of Gib-San Pools, Ltd.*

Furnishing Your Outdoor Room

The options in outdoor furniture are increasing rapidly in the market, and increasingly the furnishings mimic what is found inside the house. Thick cushions, permanent upholstery, wider chairs for longer lounging, and better, more durable finishes for longevity are among the innovations hitting the marketplace. At the end of the day, comfort and style are what will sell you on your selection of home furnishings. Local shopping or Internet surfing may prove overwhelming, though, as you confront the huge variety of products available. Besides budget and taste, one factor that can help you choose the right furnishings for your environment are maintenance and storage issues. Consider your climate, and whether your furnishings need space to store away in during the off season.

For instance, most wood furnishings, with the exception of cedar and teak, need to be stored indoors during

Bright colors and fanciful patterns draw attention to this interesting outdoor room, energizing the space. *Courtesy of Carter Grandle*

winter months, as does wicker and rattan. Cushions, umbrellas, and all outdoor fabrics should all be sheltered during seasons or extended periods when not in use to keep them clean and dry. Though many outdoor fabrics manufactured today are mildew resistant, others need to be treated with a mild bleach and detergent solution upon occasion to ward off mildew. One cup of bleach, two cups of detergent, and a gallon of water can be mixed, sprayed on the cushions or fabrics, and then rinsed with clean water and allowed to thoroughly dry. Allow all fabrics to dry completely before storing, and never store in plastic as this will prevent them from breathing.

Likewise, a mild soap and water solution can be used to clean wicker and wooden furnishings. A mild pressure wash or hosing can help, but harsh water pressure can damage the furniture.

Here's a bench built for two. Size and shape make it perfect for having a meaningful conversation or just sitting close. *Courtesy of Laneventure*

Resin and metal furnishings are the easiest to maintain, easily washed with water and gentle detergents, or a power washing for more difficult clean-ups. Though many metal furnishings are rust-resistant or rust-free, many are not and need to be protected from corrosion with wax or naval jelly.

The most important tip is to ask lots of questions of the dealer and/or manufacturer of your outdoor furniture with regard to their finishing process and recommended maintenance. Many offer product guarantees that are contingent upon the owner following their maintenance suggestions.

A carved panel and teak furnishings add an aura of tropical lush to this patio setting.
Courtesy of Harrison Design Associates

A sleek lounge chair provides a sculptural element on this minimalist patio. *Courtesy of Gloster Furniture, Inc.*

A deck springs to life with the vivid colors of upholstered, aluminum furnishings. The cast aluminum range of deep-cushion seating and tables features a durable, black powder-coated finish. *Courtesy of American Home Furnishings Alliance*

A small pergola on the back forty lures homeowners far from their distractions. *Courtesy of Laneventure*

Tightly upholstered seating heads outdoors in the groundbreaking Louis Soleil collection. Upholstery is secured to the beautiful hand-carved teak frame with weather-proof tacks. *Courtesy of Sutherland and Perennials Outdoor Fabrics*

Choosing Environmentally
Friendly Furnishings

*Re- printed with permission from the Worldwise WiseGuide at
www.worldwise.com.*

Garden furniture certainly isn't a necessity to make your plants grow, but it makes it much easier to sit and enjoy them! A well-placed bench can be a visual focal point as well as an invitation to rest. Chaise lounges and dining tables can turn a deck or patio within a garden into an outdoor room and add living space to your home.

Garden furniture is available made from a variety of materials, across a wide price range. Here is a summary of the available materials, their characteristics and environmental impacts.

IRON

Cast and wrought iron has long been used for durable garden furniture that can withstand any conditions. Iron is one of the basic elements of the Earth and is found abundantly in rocks. It undergoes little processing before being used in a variety of products. Much of the iron used in products today is recycled scrap iron.

ALUMINUM

Aluminum garden furniture is inexpensive and durable. Aluminum is a nonrenewable resource, but over 40 percent of aluminum generally available is recycled, so it is possible that any aluminum product you purchased contains recycled content, whether or not that is stated on the label. Aluminum garden furniture is made from tubular aluminum (hollow tubes that are thin and flimsy) or solid cast or wrought aluminum.

WOOD

Much of the classic-style garden furniture is made from wood. Depending on the durability of the type of wood, wood furniture can last for years before it is broken down by the elements and can biodegrade back into the Earth, making it a sustainable choice. The problem, however, is that the wood is not being grown and harvested in a way that sustains our forests. Forests are home to over two-thirds of all plants and animals on earth. They help keep our air and water clean and help stabilize the world's climate.

Good ecoforestry practices include maintaining the habitats of all native plant and animal species, maintaining a mix of trees of various ages, minimizing openings created by logging, conserving the soil by logging with light, compact equipment and minimal road building, taking only the amount of timber that will grow in the interval between harvests, making workers and local communities stakeholders and beneficiaries of forest management practices.

Ecoforestry allows us to have both the forest and the tree products, but it will succeed only if the market supports it. Look for a seal from an independent, third-party certification program to ensure that genuine ecological forest products were used. For a tree to become a finished wood product, it must pass through a "chain-of-custody," including harvest, primary and secondary processing, manufacturing, distribution, and sale. Certifiers audit each step of the process, to assure consumers that the certified products are actually produced ecologically. Operations that meet the certifying standards may display the certifier's logo.

Teak is considered to be the premier wood used for garden furniture because it is heavy, durable, rot-resistant, maintenance-free, and does not splinter. It does not have to be sealed, stained, or finished. It can be left outdoors untreated and withstand the elements for years. After a couple of seasons in the sun, teak weathers from a warm honey brown to an attractive silvery gray.

Tectona Grandis is an extremely dense hardwood of the family *Verbenaceae*. It is indigenous to India, Burma, Thailand, Indochina and Java. The harvest of teak does not destroy rain forests – it cannot even grow in rain forests. It is a deciduous tree that grows well in the dry, hilly terrain typical of plantation forests in Southeast Asia.

Much of the teak that is used to make furniture comes from very large teak plantations in Java, which were first planted by the Dutch in the early 1800s. In Java, the government agency Perum Perhutani is responsible for managing extensive forests and plantations. They operate a strict policy regulating the number and size of trees that can be felled, as well as with regard to the numbers of trees that are replanted to maintain the productivity of the teak forests for future generations. The teak plantations produce a high value crop that is a very valuable source of income in their local area. And the associated furniture and timber products industry provides regular local employment to many thousands of people. Teak can also be taken from forests, which may or may not be sustainably harvested. Be sure to find out where the teak comes from when making your selection.

Also look for good workmanship. Mortise-and-tenon joints and hand-sanded edges are evidence of a quality product. Teak furniture is expensive, but you can reduce the cost by purchasing kits to make teak furniture, rather than the assembled pieces. Also, some furniture is manufactured in America instead of Asia, which is less expensive due to savings on shipping.

Cedar. Cedar is another popular choice for outdoor furniture. It is almost half as heavy as teak, which can be a disadvantage for durability, but an advantage if you want to be able to move the furniture around easily.

Cedar contains natural oils that act as preservatives to help the wood resist insect attack and decay. It is also a dimensionally stable wood that lies flat and stays straight. Properly finished and maintained, cedar ages gracefully and endures for many years, but it does need a finish to be used outdoors.

The majority of *Thuja plicata* grows in coastal forests. Western Red Cedars grow also in the drier interior forests of British Columbia, Washington, Idaho, and Montana. They are predominantly managed forests, not wilderness. Be sure to check for certification of ecological practices, as descriptions of practices such as "reforestation program" can mean clearcutting and replanting, which is not sustainable forestry. For American gardens, cedar is a more appropriate indigenous wood than tropical teak, but less long-lasting.

Redwood. Redwood is naturally durable and resistant to decay and insects, tough enough to resist warping and splitting, and requires little or no maintenance. Redwood is native to California, and all redwood used to make products comes from California.

There are two types of redwood. The Sierra Redwood (*Sequoiadendron gigantea*), also known as the Giant Sequoia, isn't used commercially. Ninety-five percent of the Sierra Redwoods are preserved in state and federal groves. The Coastal Redwood (*Sequoia semperviens*) is used to make redwood products. While there has been much publicity about the logging of old-growth forests, now 85 percent of the state's old growth (trees over 200 years old) coastal redwoods are preserved in 350 square miles of parkland, equivalent to a one-mile wide redwood forest stretching from San Francisco to Los Angeles. None of these preserved ancient forests are used to produce lumber.

More than 96 percent of today's redwood lumber comes from lands that have been previously harvested, replanted for a second growth, and managed to ensure that redwood forests are renewed. Most redwood on the market is second and third growth redwood from lands that have been repeatedly replanted. Second growth trees are easy to regenerate (they sprout from stumps and root crowns) and grow rapidly – up to seven feet in one growing season. Given their rapid growth rate, the renewal process is very quick in comparison to other harvestable woods. Replanted forests are not always managed sustainably, however, so again, look for certification.

While most redwood furniture is made from newly-milled lumber, some smaller companies use mill ends and even redwood reclaimed from other sources. Reclaimed redwood is often from products or buildings that were originally constructed from the highest-grade old growth clear all-heart redwood, so the wood is still very beautiful and durable despite its age.

Willow. Willow branches are used to make rustic-looking bentwood furniture. Since the skinny branches generally still retain their bark, no finish is needed. Willow branches are very fast-growing and usually individually collected by hand by the craftsperson from a nearby forest. Generally these are harvested in a sustainable way, as the craftsperson has an interest in maintaining their supply.

Pine and other woods. Other woods are occasionally used for inexpensive garden furniture, but they are not a good value. Most will warp, splinter, and rot when left outdoors untreated and need toxic preservatives.

WICKER / RATTAN

"Wicker" and "rattan" are used interchangeably to describe a type of garden furniture, but each word has a different definition. Wicker simply means "a small pliant twig or branch," while rattan is the climbing palm of the genera Calamus and Daemonorops with very long tough stems. Rattan is used for "wickerwork" which is the characteristic weaving of these stems to make furniture and other household items.

While rattan is a natural, renewable resource, many wicker products are coated with finishes made from petrochemicals. If you choose wicker, check to see if it has a finish and what that finish is made from. Wicker furniture will break down when exposed to the elements in the garden, so it is not long-lasting, but it is a good choice for a renewable material that is also biodegradable.

Not all wickerwork furniture is made from rattan. There is also a "synthetic wicker" so make sure you get the real thing.

PLASTIC

The least expensive garden furniture is made from plastic. Plastic is not generally recommended as a sustainable material because it is a nonrenewable resource, toxic in its manufacture, and not biodegradable. Purchasing garden furniture and other products made from *recycled* plastic, however, is a good way to utilize plastic that is already available instead of putting it into a landfill. In addition, using recycled plastic products conserves other natural resources that would have been used instead.

Matte black patio furniture stands out on a limestone surface. *Courtesy of Carter Grandle*

Because it is so light and durable, wicker is frequently used to in the construction of outdoor furniture. Here an entire living room set has been transposed into wicker to make an outdoor living room. *Courtesy of Carter Grandle*

Furnishings set the tone in any environment, and provide a surprising place in this one. A chair wide enough to allow its occupant to tuck her legs up is one of many ways this setting has been designed to tempt lingerers. *Courtesy of Laneventure*

Bronze furnishings add aristocracy to a verandah paved in marble. Griffin statues further enhance the formal atmosphere of the room. *Courtesy of Casatta*

Outdoor Rooms | 141

Resource Guide

ARCHITECTURE

California Redwood Association
Novato, California
(415) 382-0662
www.calredwood.org

Fryday & Doyne Architecture Interior
  Design
Charlotte, North Carolina
(704) 372-0001
www.fryday-doyne.com

David Gast & Associates
San Francisco, California
(415) 885-2946
www.GastArchitects.com

Jarvis Architects
Oakland, California
(510) 654-6755
www.jarvisarchitects.com

David Lawrence Gray Architects
Santa Monica, California
(310) 394-5707
www.davidgrayarchitects.com

Harrison Design Associates
Atlanta, Georgia
(404) 365-7760
www.harrisondesignassociates.com

KAA Design Group
Los Angeles, California
(310) 821-1400
www.kaadesigngroup.com

MAK Studio
San Francisco, California
(415) 861-5646
www.makstudio.net

Shipley Architects
Dallas, Texas
(214) 823-2080
www.shipleyarchitects.com

Peter A. Zepponi, AIA Architects
San Francisco, California
(415) 334-2868
www.zepponi-architects.com

BUILDERS

Casa Decks
Virginia Beach, Virginia
(757) 523-4505
www.casadecks.com

H. Davis Construction Company
Pleasant Hill, California
(925) 674-1340
www.hdavisconstruction.com

Dream Decks
Folsom, Pennsylvania
(610) 534-9054
www.dreamdecksonline.com

Harbourside Custom Homes
Bonita Springs, Florida
(239) 949-0200
www.harboursidecustomhomes.com

McGarvey Custom Homes
Bonita Springs, Florida
(239) 992-8940
www.mcgarveycustomhomes.com

Toll Brothers
North America
(800) 289-8655
www.tollbrothers.com

INTERIOR DESIGN

Karen Black's Kitchens and Rooms by
  Design
Oklahoma City, Oklahoma
(405) 858-8333
www.karenblackskitchens.com

Susan Cohen Associates, Inc.
Santa Monica, California
(310) 828-4445
www.susancohenassociates.com

Yvonne Gregory Interiors, LLC
Mount Pleasant, South Carolina
(843) 881-6291
www.yvonnegregoryinteriors.com

Haynes Associates
Philadelphia, Pennsylvania
(215) 972-1778

Montana Ave. Interiors
Santa Monica, California
(310) 260-1960
www.montanaaveinteriors.com

Adrienne Spencer Interior Design
Lyndhurst, Ohio
(440) 446-0395
www.adriennespencerinteriordesign.com

The Uncommon Designer
Palm Beach Gardens, Florida
(561) 624-2212
www.uncommondesigner.com

LANDSCAPE DESIGN

David Bartsch
Nantucket, Massachusetts
(508) 228-7979
www.david-bartsch.com

Dan Berger, Landscape Designer
LandPlan Landscaping
Pleasanton, California
(925) 846-1989
www.landplanlandscaping.com

Cecco Trading, Inc.
Milwaukee, Wisconsin
(414) 445-8989
www.ironwoods.com

Classic Garden Design, LLC
Weston, Connecticut
(203) 226-2886
www.classicgardendesign.com

Conte & Conte, LLC
Greenwich, Connecticut
(203) 869-1400
www.conteandconte.com

Environmental Landscape Associates, Inc.
Doylestown, Pennsylvania
(800) 352-9252
www.elaontheweb.com

Julia Fogg, Landscape Architect & Garden
  Designer
London, England
+44 (0) 20 8316-6368
www.juliafogg.com

Brian Higley, Landscape Architect
Beacon, New York
(845) 831-1044
www.brianhigley.com

Inside Out
Davis, California
(530) 753-7147
www.insideoutjoni.biz

MarcoDesigns
Novato, California
(415) 898-5150

Moss Landscaping
Houston, Texas
(713) 861-5511
www.mosslandscaping.com

Joe Murray Landscapes
Tucson, Arizona
(520) 405-7478

Oslund and Associates
Minneapolis, Minnesota
(612) 359-9144
www.oaala.com

Park Slope Design
Studio City, California
(818) 788-4312
www.parkslopedesign.net

Remodeling Services
Columbia, South Carolina
(803) 765-9363
www.remodelingservicesunlimited.com

Sterling Landscape
Boise, Idaho
(208) 322-4505
www.sterlinglandscape.com

Stonetown Construction Corp.
Oakland, New Jersey
(201) 337-7773
www.stonetownconstruction.com

Zucker Design Associates
Laguna Niguel, California
(714) 478-0565
www.zuckerdesign.net

MANUFACTURERS

Alchymia Wood Fired Ovens
Kaitaia, New Zealand
+64 09 406-1903
www.alchymia.co.nz/index.htm

American Home Furnishings Alliance
High Point, North Carolina
(336) 884-5000
www.afma4u.org
www.findyourfurniture.com

Barlow Tyrie
Teakwood Outdoor Furnishings
Moorestown, New Jersey
(856) 273-7878
Chicago, Illinois
(312) 527-2397
Highpoint, North Carolina
(336) 889-7914
www.teak.com

Belgard-Permacon
Atlanta, Georgia
(770) 804-3363
www.belgard.biz

Brick SouthEast, Inc.
Charlotte, North Carolina
(800) 622-7425
www.gobricksoutheast.com

Bomanite Corporation
Madera, California
(559) 673-2411
www.bomanite.com

Brown Jordan
A Brown Jordan International Company
www.brownjordan.com

Buechel Stone Corp.
Fond du Lac, Wisconsin
(920) 922-4790
www.buechelstone.com

Carter Grandle
Sarasota, Florida
(941) 751-1000

Casatta
Miami Beach, Florida
(305) 724-4054
www.casatta.com

The Concrete Impressionist
Brooklyn, New York
(718) 677-1298
www.concreteimpressionist.com

Deckorators, Inc.
(800) 332-5724
www.deckorators.com

EP Henry Corporation
Woodbury, New Jersey
(800) 444-3679
www.ephenry.com

Empire Comfort Systems®, Inc.
Belleville, Illinois
(800) 851-3153
www.empirecomfort.com

Fogazzo Wood Fired Ovens and Barbecues, LLC
Arcadia, California
(866) FOGAZZO (toll free)
www.fogazzo.com

Gloster Furniture, Inc.
South Boston, Virginia
(888) GLOSTER
www.gloster.com

Ideal Concrete Block Company, Inc.
Westford, Massachusetts
(978) 692-3076
www.idealconcreteblock.com

Laneventure
Conover, North Carolina
(800) 235-3588
www.laneventure.com

Mutual Materials Co.
Bellevue, Washington
(800) 477-7137
www.mutualmaterials.com

O.W. Lee, Inc.
Ontario, Canada
(800) 776-9533
www.owlee.com

Oaks Concrete Products
Wixom, Mississippi
(800) 876-OAKS
www.oakspavers.com

Oldcastle Architectural, Inc.
Atlanta, Georgia
(800) 899-8455
www.oldcastle.com

Perennials Outdoor Fabrics
Irving, Texas
(888) 322.4773
www.perennialsfabrics.com

Robert H. Peterson Co./Fire Magic
City of Industry, California
(626) 369-5085
www.rhpeterson.com

Resource Guide

Santa Barbara Designs
Santa Barbara, California
(800) 919-9464
www.sbumbrella.com

Telescope Casual Furniture, Inc.
Granville, New York
(518) 642-1100
www.telescopecasual.com

TimberTech
Wilmington, Ohio
(937) 655-5222
www.timbertech.com

Trellis Structures
Beverly, Massachusetts
(888) 285-4624
www.trellisstructures.com

Tropitone Furniture Company, Inc.
Irvine, California
(949) 951-2010
www.tropitone.com

Unilock
Aurora, Illinois
(630) 892-9191
www.unilock.com

Winston Furniture
A Brown Jordan International Company
www.winstonfurniture.com

XcelDeck
Pheonix, Arizona
(800) 644-9131
www.xceldeck.com

POOLS & SPAS

Aqua Blue Pools
N. Charleston, South Carolina
(843) 767-7665
Hilton Head Island, South Carolina
(843) 680-2232
www.aquabluepools.com

Artistic Pools, Inc.
Atlanta, Georgia
(770) 458-9177
www.artisticpools.com

Creative Master Pools
Franklin Lakes, New Jersey
(201) 337-7600
www.creativemasterpools.com

Custom Pools, Inc.
Boise, Idaho
(208) 345-2792
www.custompoolsandpatio.com

Gib-San Pools, Ltd.
Toronto, Ontario Canada
(416) 749-4361
www.GibSanPools.com

Greenville Pool & Supply Co.
Greenville, North Carolina
(252) 355-7121
www.greenvillepool.com

Gym & Swim
Louisville, Kentucky
(502) 426-1326
www.gymandswim.com

Madison Swimming Pool Co., Inc.
Goodlettsville, Tennessee
(615) 865-2964
www.madisonswimmingpools.com

Memphis Pools
Memphis, Tennessee
(901) 365-2480
www.memphispool.com

Maryland Pools, Inc.
Columbia, Maryland & Fairfax, Virginia
(410) 995-6600 & (703) 359-7192
www.mdpools.com

Patio Pools of Tucson
Tucson, Arizona
(520) 886-1211
www.patiopoolsaz.com

Pool Tech Midwest, Inc.
Cedar Rapids, Iowa
(319) 365-8609
www.pooltech.com

Prestige Pools & Spas, Inc.
Edmund, Oklahoma
(405) 340-7665
www.prestigepoolsandspasinc.com

Riverbend Pools
Plano, Texas
(972) 596-7393
www.riverbendpools.com

Rizzo Pool Construction Co.
Newington, Connecticut
(860) 667-2214
www.rizzopools.com

Shasta Pools & Spas
Phoenix, Arizona
(602) 532-3750
www.shastapools.com

St. Lawrence Pools Ltd.
Kingston, Ontario, Canada
(613) 389-5510